11·50

Diary of a KICKBOXING Freak

Heinemann
LIBRARY

www.heinemann.co.uk/library
Visit our website to find out more information about **Heinemann Library** books.

To order:
 Phone 44 (0) 1865 888066
 Send a fax to 44 (0) 1865 314091
🖥 Visit the Heinemann Bookshop at www.heinemann.co.uk/library to browse our catalogue and order online.

Produced by Monkey Puzzle Media Ltd
Gissing's Farm, Fressingfield, Suffolk IP21 5SH, UK

First published in Great Britain by Heinemann Library, Halley Court, Jordan Hill, Oxford OX2 8EJ, part of Harcourt Education. Heinemann is a registered trademark of Harcourt Education Ltd.

Author: Clive Gifford
Editorial: Paul Mason
Series Designer: Mayer Media Ltd
Book Designer: Mayer Media Ltd
Illustrator: Sam Lloyd
Production: Séverine Ribierre

Originated by Repro Multi-Warna
Printed in China by WKT Company Limited

ISBN 0 431 17543 8
08 07 06 05 04
10 9 8 7 6 5 4 3 2 1

British Library Cataloguing in Publication Data
Gifford, Clive
Diary of a Kickboxing Freak
796.8'3
A full catalogue record for this book is available from the British Library.

Acknowledgements
With thanks to **Mike Duffy/Knuckles Muay Thai Ltd** for supplying all photographs, with the exception of: **front cover** supplied by **Franck Seguin/TempSport/Corbis**.

Every effort has been made to contact copyright holders of any material reproduced in this book. Any omissions will be rectified in subsequent printings if notice is given to the publishers.

Attention!

This book is about kickboxing, which is a dangerous sport. This book is not an instruction manual or a substitute for proper lessons. Get expert instruction, always wear the right safety equipment, and make sure you fight within your own ability.

CONTENTS

Kickboxing words are explained on page 30.

I AM A KICKBOXING FREAK

Jake Evans Fact File
Age: Sixteen
Years kickboxing: Two
Favourite food: Baked potato with cheese and beans
Favourite move: Spinning back-kick to head
Hobbies: Kickboxing, watching soccer – my team is Manchester United – listening to R'n'B and some rap
Pet hates: Washing my own kit after classes!

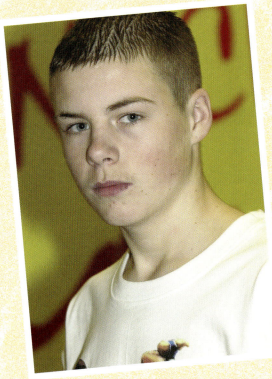

This is me!

Hi, I'm Jake Evans and I'm mad about the sport of kickboxing. Ever since I started, I've been keeping a sort of diary. Looking through, I reckon it shows the most important stages of my kickboxing career. Well, so far, anyway. I hope to go a lot, lot further. One day, I'd like to be as good as Maurice Smith, an all-time kickboxing legend and a real hero of mine. He's retired now after 20 years as a champion kickboxer so I won't get the chance to meet him in a bout. Just as well – he was awesome!

Me after a training session at the gym, with my coach and mates.

Here's me performing my favourite kickboxing move. It's called a spinning back-kick to head. It's totally hardcore.

DECEMBER

1	8	15	22	29
2	9	16	23	30
3	10	17	24	31
4	11	18	25	
5	12	19	26	
6	13	20	27	
7	14	21	28	

This is me practising fighting stance. I'm right-handed so my left foot goes ahead, toes pointing forward. My knees are slightly bent and my feet are shoulder-width apart to give me a really solid base to attack and defend from.

EARLY DAYS

I've just got back from my first-ever kickboxing class. I'm so tired I can just about lift a pen to write. I blame Erik, my penpal from Minnesota in America. He's been into kickboxing for over a year and sent me a cool DVD a few weeks back. It finally persuaded me to give kickboxing a go.

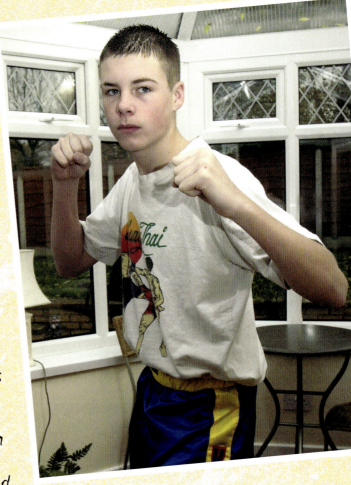

We started with about 15 minutes of warming up doing things like star jumps, running on the spot and arm circles like windmills. Then the whole class did stretching exercises. Our instructor explained that a kickboxer needs to be really flexible. Then I learned about the basic fighting stance, and we watched more advanced kickboxers practise their moves. Close up, the action looks even better than on the DVD. Everyone seemed really friendly. I can't wait to learn more!

6

Jake, this is the jab, the most common punch in kickboxing. It keeps your opponents at a distance. Erik

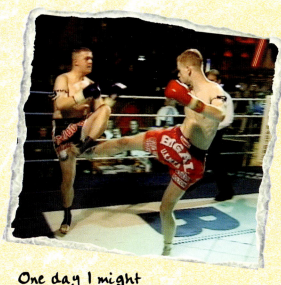

One day I might have technique like these fighters!

FEBRUARY

2	9	16	23
3	10	17	24
4	11	18	(25)
5	12	19	26
6	13	20	27
7	14	21	28
1	8	15	22	29

KICKBOXING KIT

I sent an email to Erik today to let him know how I'm getting on.

| Compose | Addresses | Folders | Options | Print | Help |
| Reply All | Forward | Delete | Previous | Next | Close |

From: Jake
To: Erik
Subject: photos
Date: Wednesday, February 25

Hi Erik,

I'm really getting into kickboxing now and here's the proof! One of my classmates, Tony, took the pics with his digital camera. You can see I've got all the kit. Well, it's not mine – I'm using the gear from the gym. My instructor says that there's no need to buy your own kit until you've gained plenty of experience. It's not cheap and you need good quality gear to protect you. The first time I put all of this gear on it felt really odd, but now I'm getting used to wearing it.

See ya!

Jake

Here's me shadow sparring – I'm trying to land an uppercut punch on an invisible chin. The training gloves have heavy padding.

8

Pads on headguards protect your cheekbones from punches and kicks. I bet this guy wishes he was wearing one!

Headguards must be worn in amateur kickboxing. I tried several on with my instructor to find a comfortable fit which doesn't restrict my view. He adjusted the headguard straps so that it doesn't slip.

Footguards and shinpads protect you when kicking. I broke my toe as a kid once, and did it hurt! I don't want to break one again...

APRIL

5	12	19	26
6	13	20	27
7	14	21	28
1	8	15	22	29
2	9	16	23	30
3	10	17	24
4	11	18	25

USING FOCUS PADS & GUARDS

Thump! Bash! Crunch! I'm no longer just practising moves in thin air. I'm starting to use focus pads and kicking shields. Focus pads are padded blocks held by our instructor, which we aim to hit with our punching moves and some kicking moves. Kicking shields are like focus pads' big brothers. They're really large pads, shaped like a rectangle. It's great to feel your kick or punch actually hit something. Connecting well gives a really satisfying thud!

Here's my kickboxing classmate, Tony, throwing a punch into the focus pads.

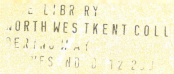

NO. 5: THE FRONT ROUNDHOUSE KICK TO HEAD

To perform this explosive kick, you do the following:

1 Lift your left leg to your chest with knee pointing to target.

2 Pivot on your right foot as you straighten your leg.

3 Rotate your hips and body too.

4 Aim to strike the target with your instep or the lower part of your shin.

Must learn this move inside out, as roundhouse kicks are used more than any other.

Here's me performing a front kick into focus pads. I've lifted the knee of my front leg and then quickly straightened my leg. I've hit the pad with the sole of my foot.

11

JULY

5	12	19	26
6	13	20	27
7	14	21	28
1	8	15	22	29
2	9	16	23	30
3	10	17	24	31
4	11	18	25	

FAST LEARNER

I don't get much praise in classes at school but I'm getting it at kickboxing. My instructor says I'm a fast learner. I reckon it's because I'm so into the sport. Mind you, there's so many moves and techniques to learn and remember. We're starting to learn how to link individual punches and kicks together quickly. These are called combinations and are really important for success in bouts.

Mum and Dad bought me my own gloves last month, which are well padded for hitting punchbags and pads. Handwraps go on before the gloves. These are long rolls of material that support the bones in your hand. They help avoid broken and chipped bones, and give your wrist support as well. Just as well: I'm starting to hit the bag with a good thump now.

HOW TO PERFORM A BASIC HANDWRAP

1 Put a loop over the thumb and start wrapping across the back of the hand and around the wrist two times.

2 Bring wrap forward and wrap knuckles two or three times to completely cover them.

3 Bring the wrap down and around the thumb, then around the wrist and back round the thumb again.

4 Bring wrap across the back of the hand and start wrapping around the hand and wrist in a figure of eight shape. Wrap remainder around wrist.

Me practising a combination. First, jabs to the head, then following up with a kick to the body with my right leg.

As you can see, kickboxing is really thirsty work! I always make sure I have a drink ready for after class.

Mum's threatened me that if my homework grades don't improve, I'll have to wash my handwraps and long pants myself!

13

SEPTEMBER

6	13	20	27
7	14	21	28
1	8	15	22	29
2	9	16	23	30
3	10	17	24	
4	11	18	25	
5	12	19	26	

IN DEFENCE

Addresses   Folder

Forward   Delete

From: Erik
To: Jake
Subject: defense!
Date: Thursday, September 23

Hiya Jakey,
Thanks for your email last week. Pleased your attacking moves are going so well. Nice to hear that you've got your rear roundhouse kick really flying. It's such a useful move. How's your defense going? I ask because my instructor reckons many kickboxers don't work hard enough on defense. These are some classic defense moves:

1 **How to block a straight righthand punch to your body:** You turn to the right and block the punch with your left elbow.

2 **Avoiding a left jab by slipping or evading a punch:** The fighter rolls his or her left shoulder forward and down, so that the punch passes over their left shoulder.

3 **Blocking a rear roundhouse kick to the left side of your head:** You step forward with your left leg and turn your left side slightly forward. At the same time, you raise your left forearm to block the kick.

4 Practise bobbing and weaving under a rope tied to the corners of your gym's boxing ring. Some photos are attached.

Good luck!
Erik

I keep my basic stance, my head level and try to make the movements flow as I dip under the rope and rise up on the other side.

Doh, Erik. We've been working on slipping punches for over two months! These girls are from my gym.

Remember: stay on the balls of your feet in defense and attack.

Blocking a high roundhouse kick in contest.

NOVEMBER				
1	8	15	22	29
2	9	16	23	30
3	10	17	24	
4	11	18	25	
5	12	19	26	
6	13	20	27	
7	14	21	28	

BRILLIANT BIRTHDAY

What a brilliant birthday! Mum and Dad have gone mental and bought me all my own kickboxing kit to go with my gloves. I kind of knew in advance as I heard Dad asking advice from my instructor after class last week. Mum and I went into town to a martial arts shop recommended by my instructor. We took time to try on different pieces of equipment to make sure they were a good fit. Mum insisted I carry all the boxes and bags myself!

What I didn't expect was back at home. Dad said I had chores to do and led me to our garage. He was right, there was work to do in the garage ... building my very own mini-gym! There's space for me to use a skipping rope for fitness, and we fixed up an old mirror on the wall so I can practise my moves. Dad bought an old punchbag on a stand, which we can put outside. He even got hold of a kickboxing poster to stick on the garage wall. How cool is that?

Inspirational garage-wall poster!

No, I'm not vain, I'm practising punching while keeping my basic stance, in front of my mirror. Using a mirror is a cool way to fight an imaginary opponent!

These fighters are older. Younger kickboxers like me don't use free weights at all.

My pal Dave trying out my punchbag with a side-thrust kick, then a punch. See how he leans backward and twists his hips to drive his leg forward into the bag for the kick.

	Download Manager		
File	Status	Time	Transfer
✓ 🌐 Kickbox info.sit	Complete	< 1 minute	1.2 MB

Choosing the Right Length Skipping Rope

A: Legs shoulder width apart
B: Stand on the skipping rope
C: Pull the handles up to your hips
D: The handles should rise just above your hipbones.

NOVEMBER

1	8	15	22	29
2	9	16	23	30
3	10	17	24	
4	11	18	25	
5	12	19	26	
6	13	20	27	
7	14	21	28	

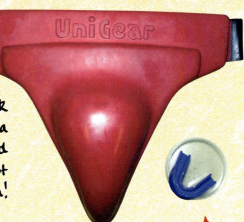

No sniggering! A kick in the groin without a groin protector would make you cry, not laugh!

I want to keep my teeth, so I'll be wearing a mouthguard even though it feels funny. Reckon I'll get used to it just like I did with the headguard.

SPARRING

Sparring with a real-life opponent is really good fun. A couple of kids in the class don't want to, so they don't have to. Choosing to spar or not is up to each person. Tony told me that some kids and adults never spar or actually fight – they just use kickboxing as a great way to keep in shape. Me, well, I couldn't wait to spar. I need hundreds of hours of sparring to get anywhere near Maurice Smith's level.

To spar we have to wear extra protective kit – a mouthguard and a groin protector. We had to buy our own mouthguards but the gym supplied groin protectors. Many girls who spar wear padded chest protectors as well. Sparring really sharpens your skills. I got caught plenty of times and was pretty sore after my first spar, but the protective gear really does its job.

Tony practising on the heavy bag.

18

Tony and I spar in the gym with our instructor not far away. The punches and kicks we use are classed on whether they're close, medium or long range.

Side-thrust kick: a long-range move.

FEBRUARY

	7	14	21	28
1	8	15	22
2	9	16	23
3	10	17	24
4	11	18	25
5	12	19	26
6	13	20	27

FIGHT NIGHT

Just got back from seeing a real kickboxing competition. Aziz, Julia, Tony and most of our class went with our instructor this evening to see some champion kickboxers in action. They were amazing. The speed and power of their kicks was awesome, and the number of punches and kicks they made in a single round made me tired watching them.

Kickboxing rules vary — there are lots of different types. The sort of kickboxing I do is amateur semi-contact. This is where kicks and punches are thrown only above the waist and protective clothing is worn. We saw two different types of bouts in the evening.

Souvenirs of a great night out. One day I hope to be in the programme as a contestant, not buying one as a spectator.

Low outside kick to the thigh in a Thai boxing bout.

An axe kick aims to land on a kickboxer's head. Needs plenty of timing and lots of flexibility to get the leg so high and then down sharply.

This looked like a destructo move!

We were all really excited about going to see the fights, even though we refused to smile for our coach when he took this photo!

Some of the contests were semi-contact but we also saw professional fighters perform Thai boxing with no headguard, bare feet and only groin protectors and mouthguards. Thai boxing allows kicks to the legs and the use of knees and elbows. It looked really, really tough.

APRIL

4	11	18	25
5	12	19	26
6	13	20	27
7	14	21	28
1 8	15	22	29
2 9	16	23	30
3 10	17	24	

Lucky I actually like cereal, toast and juice for breakfast, because that's a good healthy start for training.

THE COUNTDOWN

My first fight... it's getting close. Aziz and Julia aren't going to enter competitions and have proper fights, not yet at least. Tony and I can't wait, though. I've been training hard, getting fit running and skipping, and grooving all my moves. I'm really careful to warm up and stretch before every session. The last thing I want is an injury before my big day. I'm also trying to train my tastebuds — out are burgers and fries, at least at the moment, and in is pasta and lots of fresh fruit and veg. Mum can't believe it — she says she's been trying to get me to eat more fruit for years.

Why increase flexibility?

Flexibility gives your body's joints more range of movement. Flexibility exercises are similar to the stretches you perform during warm-up, but they are best performed after the most intense part of your workout, as your body is warm and tired and less likely to resist efforts to stretch muscles.

Got to keep up the healthy eating if I'm going to be able to do moves like this flying roundhouse.

Got the message: more flexibility = more speed and power!

BACKWARDS AND FORWARDS STRETCH

Stretch forwards and hold for a count of three or four.

SIDE BENDS

Stretch slowly to one side, hold and then do the same thing with the other side. Legs kept straight.

JUMPING SQUATS

Keep back straight. Up to 30 of these in a session to strengthen my legs. Top kickboxers can do 100 or more of these at a time and may repeat that three or four times. Ouch!

SIDE TWISTS

Twist trunk of your body to left and then right. Hands held behind head, elbows in front of chest.

LEG STRETCH SWINGS

Standing up straight, swing your leg up and out forward then move it round to the side. Always keep leg straight.

APRIL

4	11	(18)	25
5	12	19	26
6	13	20	27
7	14	21	28
8	15	22	29
1	9	16	23	30
2	10	17	24	
3			

MY FIRST FULL BOUT

I had my first actual bout three days ago – three two-minute rounds with a minute's break between. It felt so much longer. Stepping into the ring was great. I didn't feel as nervous as I thought I would – having the bout in my gym probably helped. It didn't stop me from losing though. My opponent was shorter than me but he had been kickboxing for longer and he was really good. He was always moving, and knew how to block and dodge my moves. If I caught him once with a kick or punch, I never seemed to get him with the next blow. But he managed to hit me with his combinations lots of times. I knew he'd won even before the referee lifted his hand at the end of the bout.

All that sparring in the gym with Tony was good preparation, but it didn't help me to slip many punches. I need to practise harder before my next fight!

Rick Rous (in the Stars and Stripes shorts) is a really well-known fighter. Here he's mixing an axe kick with a knee to the head.

My combinations need lots of work. I've spent some of the weekend digging out good combination moves I'm going to practise.

Tony also lost. His opponent was a girl in our class who's really fast with her moves and really strong as well. There's no trash talking or bragging in kickboxing – everyone's cool and understanding if you lose. That made it easier. Tony and I both felt the same as we left the gym. We were disappointed, but we knew we could do better with more experience.

It's a good idea to have a drink just before the headguard goes on. Not that it did me much good this time!

My mum's camerawork isn't so good. Not that I mind. At the time, I wished the camera had exploded so she couldn't record the moment. Now, I realize that losing is all part of learning how to be a better kickboxer. Best of all, I really enjoyed having a real bout, even though I lost.

MAY

2	9	16	23	30
3	10	17	24	31
4	11	18	25	
5	12	19	26	
6	13	20	27	
7	14	21	28	
1	8	15	22	29	

Me listening carefully to my instructor's last words.

MY FIRST WIN!

I enjoyed my first two bouts, at least after I got over losing them, but this was much, much better. We fought in another local gym and their instructor acted as referee. It was the best feeling ever when he told me that I'd won. Fantastic!

My combinations were tighter and faster than in the past, but my instructor reckoned it was my movement around the ring and my defence that won it for me. He says 'ringcraft' is the overall skills you have in kickboxing bouts and it only comes with experience. I know I used the ring better. Twice, I crowded my opponent into a corner where he couldn't escape a roundhouse kick and jab combination. It was great. But I remembered to be polite and respectful afterwards. Now, on to my next challenge!

What a feeling! Absolutely brilliant!

26

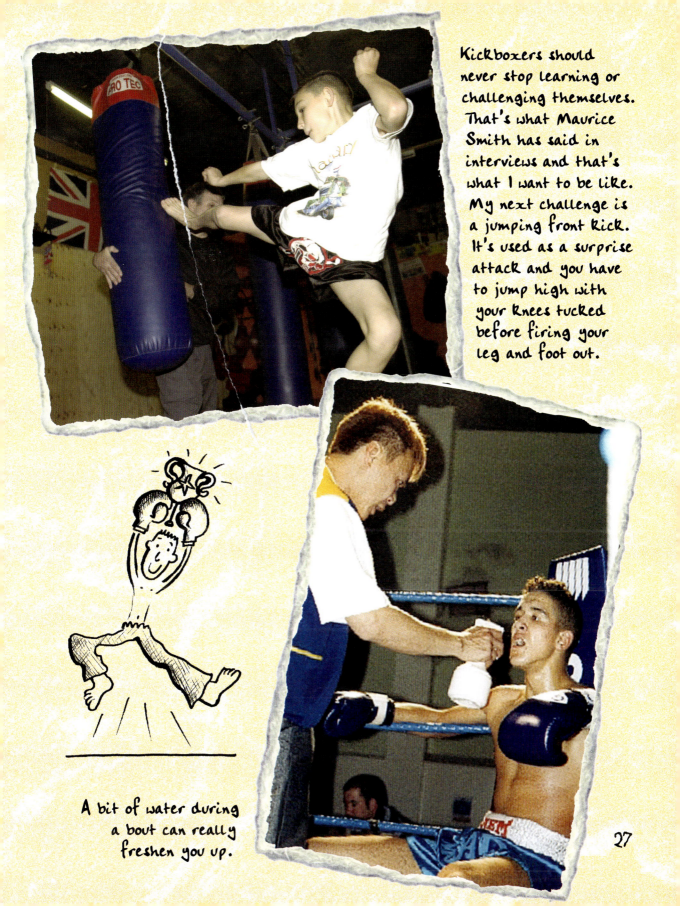

Kickboxers should never stop learning or challenging themselves. That's what Maurice Smith has said in interviews and that's what I want to be like. My next challenge is a jumping front kick. It's used as a surprise attack and you have to jump high with your knees tucked before firing your leg and foot out.

A bit of water during a bout can really freshen you up.

27

OCTOBER

	3	10	17	24	31
	4	11	18	25
	5	12	19	26
	6	13	20	27
	7	14	21	28
1	8	15	22	29
2	9	16	23	30

Showoff! A jumping side kick is used when your opponent has been hit with another kick or a punch and is moving back. Erik's got plenty of height and power in his. Looks great.

Inbox	Compose	Addresses	Folde
Reply	Reply All	Forward	Dele

From: Erik
To: Jake
Subject: defense 2!
Date: Sunday, October 30

Hi Jake,
Sorry I didn't email you earlier.
Your birthday present is in the post. It's DVD-shaped, I won't say any more. I'm really impressed that you've won your last four bouts. I told my instructor all about you. He says he's more impressed with how you reckon you've learned from your defeats and are practising your combinations. What's your record now? Nine bouts, six wins, three losses? That's real good.

I've sent you some great action shots of kickboxing legends from magazines I have, oh and one of a new legend in action! I hope to be coming to the UK on vacation in the summer and would love to stay. Maybe I can spar with you at your gym as well.

Keep kickboxing!
Erik

Maurice Smith (on the right) in action. Maurice now runs his own kickboxing center.

Earnest Hart Jr. (on the left) with the greatest champ of all, Muhammad Ali.

Ilonka Elmont (in the dark shorts and top) was born in Suriname but moved to Holland when she was thirteen. In her 30-fight career she won five world titles!

KICKBOXING WORDS

Blocking
Stopping an opponent's punches or kicks landing by using your hands or forearms as a barrier.

Bobbing
Ducking under an opponent's kick or punch.

Combination
A series of punches, and sometimes kicks, used in quick succession to weaken an opponent.

Focus pad
A practice pad that is held by a coach to allow a fighter to land blows without hurting anyone. Focus pads are used to improve technique and accuracy.

Hook
Powerful punch with a bent arm and the elbow held away from the body.

Jab
A straight, quick and sharp punch made with a straightened arm.

Kicking shield
A large pad used to practise kicks and, sometimes, punches.

Semi-contact kickboxing
A bout with punches and kicks strictly above the waist and where the fight is stopped every time a point is scored.

Shadow sparring
Practise fighting against an imaginary opponent.

Southpaw
A kickboxer who is left-handed and whose stance is the other way round from most kickboxers.

Thai boxing
This is a form of kickboxing where knees, elbows and low kicks are allowed during a bout.

TKO
Technical Knock-Out. Where a referee stops the bout because one fighter is struggling or has been knocked down three times.

Weaving
Side-to-side movement to avoid a punch or kick to the head.

INTERNET LINKS

www.kickboxing-wka.co.uk/

The homepage of the World Kickboxing Association, which is based in the UK. Clicking on the clubs link takes you to accredited kickboxing clubs and gyms in the UK and many other countries.

www.wkausa.com

The website of the World Kickboxing Association in the USA, with lots of information on the rules, upcoming events and training tips.

www.gbmaa.com/

The Great Britain Martial Arts Association, which runs courses on kickboxing and other martial arts.

www.ikfkickboxing.com/

The homepage of the International Kickboxing Federation, with lots of information on past and current championships, training and technique tips.

DVDS AND VIDEOS

The Chris Kent Kickboxing Course

(Quantum Leap Publishers) The basics of kickboxing from warming up through basic kicks, sparring, bag work and kicks and punches. Also includes highlights of a GB v USA challenge competition.

Kickboxing – New Legends 1

(Kickfighting Films) A video of famous kickboxing bouts.

BOOKS AND MAGAZINES

Kick Boxing: The Essential Guide to Mastering the Art by Eddie Cave

(New Holland Publishers Ltd, 2001)

Kickboxing Basics by Master Joe Fox and Art Michaels (Sterling Publishing, 1998)

International Kickboxer A worldwide magazine published in Australia, which includes interviews with kickboxing greats.

Martial Arts World This magazine covers all the martial arts and usually includes features on kickboxing.

WKA Worldwide Back issues of this 84-page, full-colour kickboxing magazine are available from the WKA through their website.

DISCLAIMER
All the Internet addresses (URLs) Jake has given in this book were valid at the time of going to press. However, due to the dynamic nature of the Internet, some addresses may have changed, or sites may have changed or ceased to exist since publication. While the author and Publisher regret any inconvenience this may cause readers, no responsibility for any such changes can be accepted by either the author or the Publisher.

INDEX

Titles in the *Diary of a Sports Freak* series include:

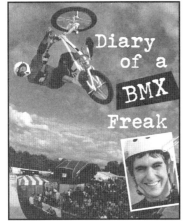

Hardback   0 431 17542 X

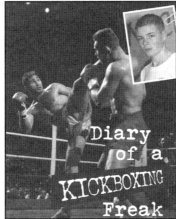

Hardback   0 431 17543 8

Hardback   0 431 17540 3

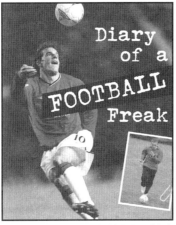

Hardback   0 431 17531 4

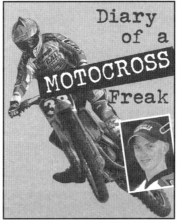

Hardback   0 431 17530 6

Hardback   0 431 17533 0

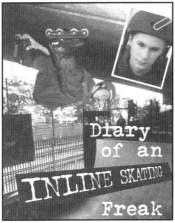

Hardback   0 431 17541 1

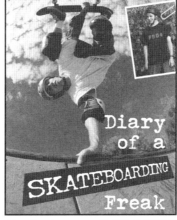

Hardback   0 431 17532 2

Find out about the other Heinemann Library titles on our website www.heinemann.co.uk/library